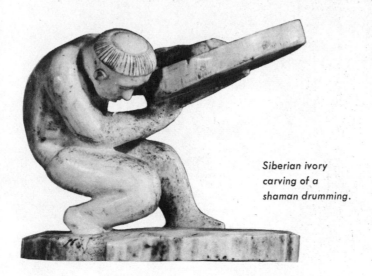

Siberian ivory
carving of a
shaman drumming.

INTRODUCING
ANIMISM

EUGENE A. NIDA
WILLIAM A. SMALLEY

ONE Introducing Animism 3

TWO Representative Animists — Dahomey 11

THREE Handling Supernatural Powers 21

FOUR Magic and Ritual. 31

FIVE Basic Animist Beliefs 50

SIX The Impact of Christianity
on the Animistic World 59

Reading List 64

FRIENDSHIP PRESS · NEW YORK

A South African witch doctor prepares a concoction to ward
off the sleep-disturbing Bird of Lightning.

African ritual drum
in the shape of a
water buffalo.

1 INTRODUCING ANIMISM

Are you an animist?

In one sense of the word you are an animist if you are a Christian, Muslim, Jew, Buddhist, Hindu, or an adherent to any religion that believes in spirit, spirits, angels, demons, ghosts, or souls. In fact, there is very little religion that does not have some animism in it, if we define animism as the belief in spirit beings. But this technical use of the word does not reflect its popular meaning. In most people's minds animism conjures up voodoo rites, secret cults, and bloody sacrifices. It stands for superstition, magic, and fear. It is restricted to "backward" and "unenlightened" parts of the globe. In this sense, are you an animist?

Not really, of course, but you, or more likely your neighbor, may have some remnants of animistic attitudes. Perhaps your neighbor believes in turning back if a black cat crosses his path. He never walks beneath a ladder and scrupulously avoids sitting at a table with thirteen people. Naturally he would never stay on the thirteenth floor of a hotel — even if there were such a floor. What is more, he may jealously guard that Indian head penny he always keeps in his wallet; he knows his lucky numbers, carries a rabbit's foot when there is something really important at stake, and likes to throw money into wishing wells. He dusts the Bible off ceremoniously every so often, for he thinks there is nothing like having a Bible around to protect his home. Perhaps he keeps an image of Saint Christopher in his car to guard against accidents. In fact, your neighbor may be one of those millions of Americans who regularly buy horoscopes to know just what to do and the auspicious time to do it. He cannot resist getting his palm read or his future told, if possible by a gypsy who uses a large crystal

3

ball. The truth of the matter is he once consulted a medium who held a seance to consult old Uncle Abner about the money that was supposed to have been left behind the chimney in the homestead.

But your neighbor is not really an animist. Even though he may believe in devils, hobgoblins, poltergeists, trolls, leprechauns, or just everyday little "meanies" called gremlins, he does not "believe" in them in the same way that an African animist believes in his spirits. This assortment of mischievous, exasperating, and unpredictable spirits does not embrace all of his life. Furthermore, your neighbor does not have the full backing of his society for his beliefs on his behavior. He is simply a marginal, superstitious fellow.

What is Religion?

All peoples have a religion, but to describe its almost infinite variety in a simple, meaningful way is almost impossible. One way to define religion is to say that it constitutes a set of beliefs about the unexpected, unpredictable, and mysterious—the uncharted region of human experience. But this is not enough, for the worshipper is himself emotionally involved in his beliefs. They are a part of him. He is struck with awe beholding the idol unveiled, and is thrilled by the touch of the god when caught up in the hysterical frenzy of a voodoo dance. Religion means action and participation, doing something about one's belief. This is true whether it is in avoiding a sacred grove of trees where Jwok of the Nilotic Anuaks is believed to dwell, or in dancing the magic drama that each year guarantees rain for the Zuni Indians of New Mexico, or leaving an offering of food each morning at a temple run by yellow robed priests of Buddhist Thailand.

Perhaps no other area of human activity has produced so many varieties of experience as has religion. Among certain tribes of Siberia the emphasis is upon good relationships with the spirits, induced by mediums who beat large drumlike tambourines, and utter mysterious words. The Melanesians of New Guinea and nearby islands are far more concerned with magic. Without it they believe they never could grow the monstrous yams that are their most valued crop, nor cast a curse upon their envied competitors. A North American Plains Indian of a century ago sought through fasting and self-torture those visions that alone could guarantee success as a great warrior or proficiency in the hunt. The Todas of South India made a religion of their dairying, for their buffaloes were almost their gods, their barns their temples, and only consecrated priests could care for the cattle.

But is there any purpose in religion? Are such beliefs, especially those of primitive peoples, of any use to them? Despite some of the obvious deficiencies, which we shall discuss later, religious beliefs do help people to have a more organized picture of the universe around them, and to visualize their relationship to the nature that is so close to them. These beliefs usually help people regulate the relationships between themselves and others. They tend to reduce fears and anxieties about the unseen and the unknown; to make people feel closer to those who have gone on before; and to provide some certainty about what awaits men after death. Religions of all kinds help to make the world a more intelligible place in which to live. "Primitive" religions of the type popularly called animistic are no exception.

What is Animism?

As already noted the precise or technical definition of animism is a belief in spirits, including the spirits of dead people as well as those that have no human origin. But on the other hand, popular usage lumps all religious practices that are not an orthodox part of the world's major faiths into the single category — animism. In our discussions of various types of beliefs we have restricted the use of "animism" to its more technical meaning. The words "animist" and "animistic" are used in a somewhat wider sense. Although they refer primarily to the central belief in spirits — a feature of virtually all primitive religions — they also include other features that almost always accompany primitive beliefs. Moreover, since this volume is intended as an introduction to primitive worship, certain practices that are not precisely animistic are also outlined.

How Widespread is Animism?

Societies in which animism in the popular sense of primitive religion is the primary or dominant form of belief include (except for those individual groups that have been converted to Christianity) the Pacific Island world, all the peoples of Southeast Asia that are not nominally Muslim or Buddhist, the aborigines of Australia, many of the hill tribes of India, Negro Africa, and the tribal groups of Siberia, and North and South America. In addition, however, even where some of the "higher religions" are the official religions of the land, the beliefs of the common people are essentially animistic. This is true of many parts of Asia, North Africa, and in nominally Roman Catholic Latin America.

A common saying in Southeast Asia is "Scratch a Muslim Javanese and you find a Hindu. Scratch the Hindu and you find a pagan." This is just another way of saying that underneath the forms of the "higher religions" there is a pagan substratum, which in many situations is actually the most important element in the religious life of the people. Underlying the Buddhism of Asia one can often find unmistakable idolatry, spirit houses, the terror of ghosts, and belief in a flaming hell. Yet all of these practices would have been utterly unacceptable to Buddha himself. Similarly, a Muslim may claim that he believes only in the will of Allah, but that does not prevent most West African Muslims from wearing charms imprinted with words of the Koran, placating the malicious jinns, or propitiating the village spirits with sacrifice. Such inconsistency should not be surprising for it occurs in all religions. Even in Christianity many believers indulge in practices that are utterly contradictory to the teaching of the Scriptures. They take oaths, kowtow to men of wealth, and show by racial prejudice that they are "respectors of persons." Scratch many an American and you find a pagan, too.

How Animistic Are the Higher Religions?

Buddhism began as a kind of protest against the mushrooming idolatry of Hinduism. Buddha called upon the people to reject pagan superstitions, to overcome ignorance by knowledge, and to defeat evil desires by self-control in order to escape from the cycle of rebirths

The Devil's dance of Oruro,
Bolivia, is sharply marked by
animistic symbols and practices.
Demon-masked dancers, left,
portray the fight of the devil
against the archangel Michael.
The black feathered condor,
right, represents
Diablada himself.

Grotesque demons,
figures from an
ancient animism,
surround and tempt a
Tibetan Buddha, below.

into the nothingness of nirvana. But the average Buddhist in Burma today understands precious little of this highly philosophical outlook; for him the countless spirits, called *nats*, are far more important. The people have their own little shrines to the *nats*. Many villages provide special places for *nat*-worship, and even in some of the Buddhist temples one may make offerings to the spirits. The annual Burmese Water Festival and the Festival of Lights are essentially institutions of *nat*-worship, although they have been officially incorporated within the country's Buddhist observances.

The Laotian people, who are also Buddhist, are thoroughly immersed in spirit worship. In Vientiane, capitol of Laos, a buffalo must be sacrificed each year near a large stone symbolizing a grain of rice. Water is then poured over this stone by a "spirit possessed" woman. The way in which the water flows over the face of the stone guides people in the placement and irrigation of their rice paddies. In the city of Luang Prabang, elephants are ridden about three times a year to the three different Buddhist temples. At the gates of these temples, men with special religious powers officiate at ancient altars with offerings of candles, betel nut, tobacco, and rice wine and whisper charms into the ears of the elephants.

One might presume that, under the fiercely anti-idolatrous banner

of Islam, the animistic practices of primitive religions would be wiped out, but such is not the case. In Indonesia, the ancient pagan spirits were given Hindu names during the period of Hindu influence. Later, when Islam was brought in, again by merchants from India, these same spirits acquired Arabic names. Present-day Javanese have hosts of *yang*. Some of these spirits protect villages, others are the spirits of the founders of the village; still others are giants and devour heavenly bodies at the time of an eclipse. The *yang* are everywhere; bits of dead wood floating in creeks are their homes. A passing spirit may blow on someone, causing him to fall ill with dysentery; a cholera plague is evidence that the spirits are at war among themselves. In some of the Javanese mosques, one can find a special place where offerings to the spirits may be made.

In the Middle East, the citadel of Islam, the jinns, which are a basic part of Islamic belief, continue to usurp people's primary loyalty to Allah. The spirits are far more numerous than people. They may be seen in mosques, are reputed to love to study the Koran, and are addicted to black magic. Jinns can, however, be made to flee by reciting the phrase, "In the name of Allah, the merciful and compassionate," and are also repulsed by herbs, gunfire, iron and salt.

In Latin America, many Roman Catholic churches are built over

Today meets yesterday as Canadian teenager, left, sketches Indian mountain lion totem over grave of one of her ancestors.

Many Japanese believe that a climb to the top of sacred Mt. Fuji will purify soul and body. Youngsters, right, clad in traditional black and white of the religious pilgrim begin their training for later summit climb.

pagan altars, and it is not uncommon in rural Mexico for the emblems of the sun and the moon to be carved into the stone over the church doorways. In Cuba, rites under the patronage of Santa Barbara take a bizarre form involving the West African god Shango, with fetish stones, the head of a goat and a rooster, drums, dancing, and a considerable measure of sex license. A similar situation exists in Haiti, although the practices here are without the official cooperation of Roman Catholic authorities. The average voodooist, if he can procure some of the consecrated wine or wafers from the mass, believes that he has a fetish of superior strength.

Animism and the Challenge to the Church

Despite the many centuries during which magic, witchcraft, and spirit worship have dominated the tribal peoples of the world, primitive religions are breaking down rapidly. The impact of scientific knowledge, the appeal of materialism, and the disruption of village life in which animistic worship is nurtured have all contributed to the rapid disintegration of animistic beliefs and practices. When a Congolese lad leaves his jungle village to find work in a factory in Leopoldville, his former offerings to the ancestral spirits seem much less important than possessing new clothes, a bicycle, or attending the cinema. When a West African Kissi, drawn by the gaudy life of the provincial capitol, finds work in the city of Kankan, he also finds himself in the shadow of the minaret. Constantly called by the mullah to prayer, he is pressured by his associates and often his boss to lay aside his animistic beliefs and to confess the claims of Islam. A Lahu tribesman in Southeast Asia who comes down to the city from his mountain home will almost inevitably have his spirit beliefs challenged by clever Communist propaganda. When confronted by the claims of materialism and well-organized systems of belief, the animist usually discovers that the faith and values of his fathers cannot be applied to the new world in which he finds himself.

What does the church say to the millions of people (perhaps more people than at any other time in world history) who are now in the very process of changing their life allegiances? Is there any message in the gospel of Jesus Christ that provides a satisfactory answer to the conflicting claims thrust upon the emergent animist? Yes! But we must examine the animist's beliefs more closely if we are to understand him, or appreciate the unique distinctiveness and extraordinary appeal that Christ has for him.

Australian "pointing bone"
is used to produce death
spell on an enemy.

2 REPRESENTATIVE ANIMISTS – DAHOMEY

Dahomey, on the coast of West Africa, has a long and fascinating history. Until this populous and colorful country was conquered by the French in the nineteenth century, the kings of Dahomey ruled over a country that in size, political authority, and cultural complexity was equivalent to many of the kingdoms of Europe in the Middle Ages. The descendants of the original people live on today with most of their culture intact, except as they have added certain of the white man's gadgets and ways.

Dahomean religion has a pantheon to rival the ancient Greeks, a world of other spirits and deified ancestors, and hosts of ordinary, faithful, busy priests, priestesses, and diviners. Its beliefs and practices are representative of a flourishing and highly developed animism.

Dahomean Souls

The average Dahomean is not quite sure just how many souls he has, although he knows very well that he has more than one. According to the best-informed people, many men have four souls, while women have three. The first, the guardian soul, is inherited from an ancestor. An observer can often tell from which ancestor this soul has been inherited by the resemblance of the individual to his ancestor. When there is no clear resemblance, a diviner must be consulted to determine the source.

The second soul is the personal soul, sometimes described as the person's voice, which more than anything else is thought to characterize an individual. When the voice leaves the body, the person dies. This soul corresponds somewhat to our idea of personality.

The third soul is a small piece of the creator that exists in every person's body. The goddess who created the world is supposed to send a little bit of herself to each person so that she can keep some control over people on earth. When a person dies this soul is taken back by the goddess.

The fourth soul, which is one's destiny or fate, is acquired only by a person who has undergone certain elaborate ceremonies. This soul is not concerned merely with the welfare of the one who possesses it, but also governs the destinies of all other members of the man's household. Good fortune and misfortune in various forms are thought to be stored in pairs of gourds and it is the business of this soul to select only good for the man and all his family. If for some reason this soul fails him, its owner must implore the guardian soul to intercede on his behalf.

The Animist Looks at Human Nature

The Dahomean's belief in several souls is, of course, peculiar to Dahomey. There are, however, some important concepts about human nature and personality that many animistic peoples share. Moreover, these views about the psychological make-up of man are fundamental. According to the Semang of Malaya, it is the soul that actually performs the deeds of which a man dreams. This same part of the personality may depart when a person faints. If the medicine man is not summoned or the magic words are not recited soon enough, the person will die.

In other areas, souls may be likened to little men who stand within people. They may be located in the eye, heart, liver, or in the kidney fat, as some Australian tribes believe. They can often be seen, for they appear in dreams and visions and are not infrequently viewed as ghosts wandering about in the forests, especially after the possessors have died. A dead man's soul may be wanting another body in which to live, or he may want to take a slave with him to the next world.

For most animists, an important fact about souls is not just that each person has at least one, without which he will sicken and die, but that such souls live on after death. A soul after death is often a major concern, for such a soul must be cared for properly. If a man possesses great power while he is alive, how much more powerful he becomes once he enters the spirit realm! One need not be too concerned about the departed spirits from good families whose living members will provide all the necessary rites to speed the spirit-soul on to the next

Blood and feathers are placed on sacred stone
as West African sacrifices chicken to guardian spirit.

world. But what about those who died by accident and whose bodies
were never recovered? These spirits may be embittered by their lot
and may try to re-enter this life. Some woman may have died without
having children, and she will probably want to kidnap the soul of a
child. Criminals may have been tortured to death and their bodies
exposed to be eaten by hyenas and buzzards. One must surely have
protection against these spirits. The Semang people greatly fear
bachelor ghosts, for in the spirit world they will have no wives unless
they capture them from the world of the living.

Worship of Ancestors

When a Dahomean dies, his personal soul, which is described as his
voice or personality, is believed to take a trip to the land of the dead.
On the road there are many obstacles that the living relatives must
prepare for if the soul of the dead person is to reach his destination.
The soul of the dead must cross several rivers and boatmen have to

be paid to ferry it across the waters. Money is given to the first boat-man, tobacco is provided for the second, and a special funeral cere-mony is performed to call the third boatman. If these rites are not properly carried out, the departed soul cannot cross the rivers and is forced to wander about, a restive, evil spirit, bringing vengeance on his neglectful offspring.

Once in the world of dead souls, a new soul joins his relatives who preceded him there. If, however, his family remaining on earth does not show proper respect for him by ceremonially deifying him, he can be expected to show his displeasure by causing illness or other misfortune. Then the family must go to a diviner to find out the cause of the misfortune. At his direction relatives begin the ceremonies to deify the departed ancestor, and to worship him regularly along with others. Although the Dahomeans have many and powerful gods, this does not diminish in any way the necessity of bestowing proper wor-ship on dead ancestors.

In some primitive societies the worship of one's ancestral spirits is the dominant theme, even more than among the Dahomeans. The Bakongo of southern Congo respect a creator god such as Nzambi Mpungu; nonetheless, all benefits are believed to come from one's good ancestors. On the other hand, care must be taken of the spirits of those who died in war, by murder or suicide, and of the spirits of sorcerers and worthless folks. However, to insure continued benefits of game, fertility, and good fortune the ancestral spirits must be entreated and placated. As one symbol of reverence, the Bakongo keep a small fire burning in a hut in the cemetery, reminding the spirits that they are not forgotten.

Among the Manus of Melanesia each head of a household had traditionally a kind of personal spirit from the world of the dead; in fact, he was the ghost of his own father, who was respectfully called "Sir Ghost." As a symbol of his presence, the father's skull was duti-fully kept hanging in the hut. Sir Ghost was an important factor in the heir's life, for he was the source of prosperity and success. But, he was also a hard taskmaster. He punished his ward if he was lazy, made him sick if he defaulted on debts, and hounded him with bad luck if he violated any of the tribal taboos. But a man could scarcely afford to kick out his own Sir Ghost, for then he would be at the mercy of myriads of evil spirits, with no one to plead his cause or ward off trouble.

There is, however, one significant and reassuring characteristic of most disembodied spirits. They do not last forever, at least in a harmful state. Either they are reborn in children (the Baganda believe that after two years spirits of the dead are re-incarnated in a baby, which must be named in honor of the ancestor) or they gradually fade away, even as they are lost to memory. But one is never quite sure when some "never-say-die" ghost will come trudging back to get in a last good lick at humanity.

The Gods

Dahomeans are well endowed with gods. Instead of having one set of gods as in most religions, they have three, each with its pantheon of deities and distinctive theological system, but all intricately interrelated. The systems are, however, so complex that only from the priests of a single group of gods can one get a clear picture of the characteristics of those particular deities. Other people may know something about the spirit beings, but their ideas are hazy and their beliefs often contradictory.

One group of Dahomean gods consists of the sky deities. They include Mawu, the creator goddess, and Nan-Baluku, who created Mawu and her twin brother Lisa. Mawu herself is the moon and Lisa the sun. She is cool and refreshing, while he is hot and feverish. She is tranquil and he is restless. She represents love and pleasure, but he, toil and war. In Mawu is concentrated the wisdom of the world, and in Lisa its strength.

Eleven other deities belong to this group of gods. They are children of Mawu and Lisa, and among them are the gods of iron, the hunt, and the keeper of the drinking water.

The other pantheons of Dahomean gods are the earth gods and the thunder gods. These groups of gods are also related to the sky gods, as are their offspring, but they comprise separate systems of deities with their own priests and priestesses, their own worshipers, and their own rites.

It is interesting to note that in many instances primitive peoples believe in a single "high god"— one who is in theory, but not in practice, equivalent to the God of Christianity. Though the people may claim that he created the world, he is seldom regarded as all-powerful. He is a sort of first-among-equals among the various gods. Generally he is far removed from people and often not worshiped in any shrine, or honored by any gifts. In West Africa a variety of myths are told in an attempt to explain this strange aloofness: (1) A woman was pounding grain and reached so high with her pestle that she struck

Renowned as bear worshipers, Ainu men and women of northern Japan here propitiate the spirit of a spherical aquatic weed, the *marimo*.

god in heaven who, in anger because she refused to stop, got up and left. (2) People kept wiping their dirty hands on the sky, which was much lower in those days, so god left in disgust. (3) People used to insist on sending smoke up into god's eyes, and he just could not stand it. (4) The people did not like to have god so close by, so they departed for a distant country.

One might think that the greatest god would be the most popular, but this is not the case in most primitive religions. Of all the gods, the most popular is usually either the god or goddess of fertility (here lies the mystery of birth, the future of the race, and the supply of food), or the culture hero, often a messenger of the gods. Among the Ibo in West Africa the nearest and dearest of all the deities is probably "the Great Mother Goddess," spirit of fertility, in whose honor each year all the mores of the tribe are cast aside for a period of sexual license.

Another favorite deity of West Africa is Legba, as he is known in Dahomey. He is a tricky, mischievous but not diabolical god, who must always be called on to carry messages to the other gods and therefore must be worshiped in any ceremony. Moreover, if he is properly propitiated, he even can be counted on to change the message from the gods in favor of the people. Despite his unpredictable tendency to mischief, he really likes people and will usually take their side. For these reasons Dahomeans, irrespective of what pantheon of gods they may worship, always pay their respects to Legba. No offering, however small, can be given to any god without a portion being dedicated to this indispensable messenger.

Other Spirits

In addition to the gods, Dahomeans also believe in other kinds of spirits that are worshiped and feared in varying degrees. One such spirit, which is very powerful, is the serpent. He manifests himself in all long, sinuous objects: the rainbow, roots of trees, nerves of animals, and the umbilical cord — symbol of fertility and life. The spirit of the serpent, believed to be utterly unforgiving, is greatly feared.

Though Dahomeans have a number of spirits, they possess nothing like the abundance of spirits with which animists usually populate the realm of nature. There may be spirits in the trees, rivers, hills, or odd-shaped rocks. Hordes of spirits may lurk at dangerous spots on the trail or in dark places in the jungle. There are endless types found the world over: those which guard the person, family, tribe, or village; those which preside over nature; demons that are constantly seeking to get into people and to cause them harm; elves that mischievously mislead people in the forests; and goblins that haunt houses and drive people mad. But there are many more kinds. In fact, the Ifugaos in the northern part of the Philippines know of more than 1,500 such spirits, each with a special name, such as Flying Monster, Deceiver, Thunderer, Gentleness. For success in any undertaking, one must know the right name and call on the right spirit at just the right time.

There are at least five important kinds of spirits:

1. The creator spirit of spirits.
2. The chief spirits, usually with special responsibilities for earth, sky, sea, animal life, fire, etc.
3. The deified ancestors, who are not just temporary ghosts, but have taken their place among the permanent spirits in charge of the world.
4. Evil or mischievous spirits, often including the culture hero, or some spirit who defied the gods to bring the people the benefits of fire, pottery, archery, etc.
5. The relatively insignificant spirits of forest, field, and stream who have mostly nuisance value, but who can give one a scare if they are not treated with respect.

But if the different types of spirits are almost innumerable, their size and shape are even less classifiable. The Arapesh of Melanesia, for example, are haunted by Marselai, who can take the form of a brightly colored, double-tailed, double-headed lizard; a one-legged kangaroo; a pig with bushes growing out of its back; or of a rat with a phosphorescent rump.

In general, the animist looks upon the spirits as he would people, recognizing their limitations, their unpredictability, their capacity for deception, and their greed for gifts. He is more concerned with the evil spirits than with the good, even as in life he finds that he must be more cautious in his dealings with bad men than with good. He is far more anxious to placate the evil spirits that may do him harm than to honor the good spirits who might help him. Furthermore, the spirits that are nearby occupy more of his attention than the deities that are far removed.

Mana: Inherent Power

In addition to an elaborate system of spirit beings, Dahomey religion is also concerned with objects that have powerful magical properties of their own. One example is a small pot with strings of raffia tufted around it to form a skirt. Over the mouth is a piece of cloth with a projecting white feather. The purpose of this charm is to protect a household when the man of the house is on a journey, and to keep the women at home faithful to him during his absence. No menstruating woman may touch the charm for fear of dire consequences — a common taboo for sacred or powerful objects. There is no spirit dwelling inside the jar. The jar alone and the words recited over it are believed to have the power to accomplish the desired end. There are scores of other such objects, each with its own distinctive power.

Primitive peoples almost everywhere regard many objects as possessing inherent power. This power is just as real a quality as size, shape, and color. It cannot be seen, but it can be tested. If a man finds a strange, unusual stone, plants it in his garden, and the next year has an abundant crop of yams, here is proof that the stone has inherent power, or "mana," as the Polynesians call it. This supernatural force may be likened to electricity that may be concentrated in some object (in fact, stored up in such quantities that for a common man to touch the object would mean instant death) and that may pass from one object to another. Almost anything is believed to have mana by one society or another: a spear which has been used to kill a large animal;

A West African fish totem, left, traditionally worn by dancers for hundreds of years, makes its transition into the modern world in the shape of an airplane, above.

a poison arrow effective against a chief; the skull of a powerful medicine man; the clothes of a king; a fleet horse; a magic formula; a secret symbol; or the ground-up horn of a wild rhinocerous. In fact, many people have mana in themselves. This is especially true of warriors and sorcerers; how would they have ever become so great without mana? Moreover, in some cases this power may be passed on by the parents and thus a child may have more than either parent alone. In the case of a dispute, such children can oust their parents from home by pronouncing a taboo upon the house.

So potent can mana be that people must be protected against it. In the past, any offering to the king of Siam had to be passed to him on a golden platter so that men would not indirectly touch royalty and thus be overcome with its power. But so much power can work two ways. One Siamese queen fell into a canal and drowned in the presence of a throng of people because no one dared to rescue her. To have touched royalty would have been a most awful transgression.

Totem: The Kinship of Man with Nature

Dahomean society is divided into thirty-nine or more groupings based on actual or imaginary family relationships. Children belong to the same grouping as their father. The mother normally belongs to a different grouping because members of the same group, considered to be related, do not intermarry. Each of these Dahomean relationships has a tradition of having been started by some non-human creature — usually an animal that married a woman. The ruling family, for example, is thought to be descended from the union of a leopard with a woman. Called the "leopard children," the members of the group do not eat the meat of the leopard, spotted antelope, or any other spotted animal that resembles the leopard.

In some groups the mythical non-human ancestor from whom people claim descent remains a guardian force for the family or clan. Such a totem may be a bear, lion, kangaroo, butterfly, spider, moth, eagle, berry bush, or cactus. Any plant, animal, insect, or in some tribes, a geographical location, may be a totem by which the clan proclaims its origin, procures a guardian, and establishes a system of relationships.

This relationship is very important in many areas. In various tribes of the Sudan, for example, it is said to be quite unknown for a crocodile to eat a member of the crocodile clan. There is a legend that on one occasion a crocodile did drag a member of the crocodile clan into the water but soon released him with only a minor wound. Similarly, a member of the scorpion clan is believed able to pick up scorpions without being stung by them. Members of such clans do not usually tempt their animal relatives by undue familiarity, but there is no doubt about the strength of their feeling for their totem.

Among the tribes of Australia totemism has received its most elaborate development, for each of life's relationships and loyalties has been symbolized by totems. For one thing, each person inherits a totem from his father, relating to the place where he was conceived. Another totem comes from one's mother and represents her clan. Still another totem is possessed by the marriage group to which each person belongs, and in addition to all this, a person can have a special, private totem.

Animists do not worship their totemic animals, although they are so closely affiliated with them. Most, like the Dahomeans, will not eat or kill them, and if they do, it is only after or with proper ceremonies of expiation. They often call themselves by the name of their totems, even as we indulge in a present-day survival of totemism when we talk of the California Bears, the Michigan Wolverines, and the St. Louis Cardinals.

Australian sacred stone
represents the spirit
of its owner.

3 HANDLING SUPERNATURAL POWERS

Of the many Dahomean religious ceremonies, one ritual in the series required for the deification of a family's ancestors may be selected as representative. In this ritual the priest of the cult of the ancestors is in charge. He first asks for the names of the dead. This is an important and dangerous question, for all of the names of the family dead must be accurately recited and none forgotten, or dire consequences will result. Before the ceremony continues the priest is given gifts of pots and gourds, as many mats as there are souls to be recalled, sixteen goats, 241 chickens, and lengths of white cloth, forty-one yards long.

Afterwards, the family assembles with faces, arms, and breasts daubed with white clay and bound with strands of raffia. They proceed to the river, with all of the pots, cloths, and gourds that have been given to the priest. There they sacrifice two goats and seven chickens while chants are sung to the accompaniment of rattles and gongs.

The chief priest then walks out into the water, and as the name of each of the dead is called out, he quickly scoops up water in one pot and covers it with another pot held in the other hand. Then the crowd is dismissed and a secret ceremony is conducted at the river by the priest and his assistant.

Outside a house, newly-constructed for the purpose, the family waits for the ancestors to come. At last, the priest comes back empty-handed and announces that the pots are now in the house. Immediately, the family goes in and finds them there. This is considered a miracle, and the people shout the praises of the priest and prostrate themselves in front of him. Animals, figurines, and other valuable gifts are given to him before he leaves.

A Japanese shinto shrine, with characteristic good luck symbols, is transported through the street as part of a festival to dispel evil spirits.

By means of this and other rituals, Dahomeans believe that they can ward off possible evil from the spirit world, and also guarantee positive benefits.

The animist, whether in Dahomey or elsewhere, does not regard himself as unable to do anything about the supernatural powers and spirits that threaten his world. Fortunately, rather than seeing himself as a passive victim of the spirit world, he believes he can use spirit forces for his own benefit. To do this, he can employ a number of means: magic words, blood sacrifices, costly offerings, elaborate ceremonies, careful avoidance, valued charms, powerful fetishes, and symbolic designs.

The Power of Words

Without doubt the most important and useful technique for controlling mana and propitiating the spirits is the use of words. These words may either be magic incantations like "hocus pocus dominocus," or prayer. Magic words may be used to make crops grow, curse an enemy, bless a friend, produce good luck, or ward off evil. In general, such magical formulae are meant to control the inherent power in some object, or they may constitute mana in and of themselves. This is why in Dahomey a vicious gag used to be put in the mouths of criminals to keep them from cursing the king. In the Ashanti empire a knife was thrust through the cheeks of criminals as they were being led away to execution lest in their anger they utter a curse, the words of which would have power in themselves to destroy. On the other hand, words are often regarded as means of petitioning the spirits, either by informing them of the sad state of affairs (in which case they are supposed to respond automatically to the need), or by pleading with them to rescue their worshipers from the threat of plague, war, or famine. Such prayers may, of course, be either informal and spontaneous or formal and ritualistic. Most animists seem to believe that the latter become more powerful by each use. In fact, some peoples believe that if prayers are repeated perfectly and often enough, the spirit must accede to the request.

But words are dangerous things to utter. You may speak of death, and a friend may die — the word has killed him. Therefore, it is especially important to avoid powerful words when talking of powerful persons or spirits. In West Africa there are a number of indirect ways of talking about what is potentially dangerous. When, for example, a king dies, one says in Abomey "it is night"; in Porto Novo, the expression is "the house is broken"; in Ashanti, "a mighty tree has been uprooted"; in Oyo, "he has entered the vault"; and in Yoruba, "a leaf has fallen." All of these denote death, but none of them use the mana-filled word.

Australian aborigines imitate locusts as part of a ceremony to increase the supply of this important item of their diet.

Offerings and Sacrifices

Words, however, are cheap both with men and the gods. Often, if one is really to show respect and win favor, he must give gifts: a little beer poured on the ground to the ancestors in central Africa; the first fruits of the rice crop to the spirit of the rice paddy in Southeast Asia; and cooked rice and vegetables placed along the watercourses for the returning spirits of the dead in Japan.

One of the problems that faces the animist is just how he can send offerings to the dead or to those in the spirit world, for ghosts and spirits obviously do not partake of food as we do. But, although the ghosts and the spirits do not eat the food, they may partake of its essence. They consume the vital force of it, especially that part that can nourish spirits. The worshiper can be sure that the offering reaches the dead if it is ceremonially killed.

When the ancient Mayas wished to cast offerings into the sacred cenote in honor of their gods, they first "killed" them. Beautiful pottery was broken, jadite-studded jewelry was smashed, and rich vestments were torn. If an animal or person is to be offered to the spirit world, it too must be killed, and at least the blood (in so many religions the symbol of life) must be sprinkled or poured on some holy object.

In many instances the god is offered the blood and the life-essence of the animal, while the people feast upon the body. But if the people wish further to impress the deity, they often burn the sacrifice completely, thus permitting smoke to take the spiritual substance of the animal into the spirit realm. If, after all this, the god still does not act, the people may conclude that either he has met resistance from a more powerful deity, or, in some societies, they may decide to give him a lesson or two. Many Ecuadorian Quechua Indians, for example, take out the image of their god and whip it for having failed them.

Ceremonies

Another way to control mana and to propitiate the spirit world is through ceremonies, some of which, as in the case of the Zuni rituals, are designed to keep men on good terms with the gods. That is to say, they are preventive rituals, planned to avert trouble before it has a chance to begin. Others may propitiate angry spirits, while others may be almost purely magical. Some of the Australian aborigines, for example, act out with remarkable realism the process by which the witchetty grubs break out of their crysalis. This is a kind of magical exhortation for the witchetty grubs to increase and thus provide the people with more food.

Taboos

One way to keep out of trouble is to avoid it. Hence, when there is some object with too much mana, one simply must not touch it or come near it. It is taboo. This, of course, can be very handy. In many parts of Polynesia, with the help of a medicine man who is an expert in such matters, one can make a taboo out of coconut fronds to keep people out of one's garden.

But taboo works two ways. If something is too holy, if it has too much spirit power, or mana, it must not be touched. If one wishes to keep his own holiness, he must not touch objects which are "unclean" or "common," for such an act would drain off sacred power. It was for this reason that, prior to the collapse of the Hawaiian native religion in 1819, the king regularly married his own sister. His person was too filled with mana for anyone else to touch, and, moreover, to marry a commoner would have been dangerous for the king himself.

Charms and Fetishes

In order to be protected from unfriendly supernatural powers, the animist may use charms that have enough mana to ward off evil, or fetishes in and through which a spirit may lend a helping hand.

For West Africa, some of the strongest charms consist of words of the Koran written on small pieces of paper that are neatly folded inside of little leather packages. These are similar to the phylacteries mentioned in the Bible. Among the Mazatecs of Mexico, a favorite charm is a jaguar claw. In other parts of the world, a charm may consist of a small bit of wild buffalo horn—for protection, the teeth of a lion—for strength, a little package of gunshot—to prevent accidents, or a miniature knife—to guard against wounds.

Such charms, or amulets, as they are also called, have power in and of themselves, and may be procured by almost anyone. However, if some important medicine man has performed the proper ceremonies over them, they become still more powerful.

Another type of spiritually powerful object is not for general use. Such are the paraphernalia of the medicine man himself: his bag of medicines, rock crystals, staff, rattle, pieces of jade, skin on which he kneels, mask that he wears, and the pebbles that he employs in

divining. In fact, these objects have so much mana that the average person, in some areas, is afraid to touch them; although some daring souls, in order to procure a super-charm, have run off with the sorcerer's own tools. They usually do so at the risk of their lives.

A charm is regarded as very effective for many of the emergencies of life, but the spirit that is associated with a fetish can usually do much more than a mere charm. For example, the Bakongo people have a famous fetish called Nkosi, the Lion, consisting of a statue, representing the male part of the fetish, and a bag, representing the female part. The bag contains such things as red and yellow clay, head and claws of an eagle, tails of a ferret and wildcat, and hair and claws

26

Animists are not always as happily free of fear as this Indonesian weaver and her daughter seem to be, left. Heavily carved symbols protect their home from evil spirits.

The little West African boy, right, has recently recovered from an illness. White symbols have been painted on his face and body to ward off any further attacks of evil.

of a lion. This fetish can be called upon to seek out thieves. First, it must be taken to the scene of the crime and then properly "awakened" with an explosion of gunpowder, sprinkled with blood, and finally spit upon by people chewing kola nuts. After apprehending the thief, the fetish is supposed to make him so ill that blood runs from his nose—a sure sign that either the thief or a member of the thief's family has been taken by Nkosi.

A further type of powerful object is an image. This is only a representation of a deity and not an idol, which would be an image indwelt by the god himself. Many images acquire considerable mana, and in some instances they are given such power from the very start. For example, most images of Buddha, especially those in important shrines or temples, are thought to contain a part of Buddha's body: a tooth, a lock of hair, a piece of bone. It is this substance that communicates mana to the image. The image becomes a dispenser of benefits to true worshippers and of curses to those who might commit sacrilege.

Some images become idols. This happens when they cease to be representations of spirit power and become that power in their own right. In Latin America many of the Indians regard the images of the Virgin in the various cathedrals as being not just representations of the mother of Jesus, but as having distinct powers in and of themselves. Each image of the Virgin has its own power: one is good if the child is sick; another is effective in curing tuberculosis; and still a third is a charm against the evil eye. When each image thus acquires special powers, one can be certain that the images are no longer mere representations, but fetishes—or idols.

Symbolic Designs

In many regions there is power in a symbol, regardless of how or where employed. The crescent of Islam, the eight-spoke wheel of Buddhism, the phallic symbols used by many tribes—all these have power to ward off evil or to bring good. For this reason they are not only painted on houses, embroidered on cloth, but are often cut right into the body, or tattooed. In Laos, people who want special protection against evil spirits will have an expert prick designs on their stomach and thighs, rubbing in a substance made from the gall of pigs and fish and mixed with soot from sesame oil lamps.

The Role of Specialists

Obviously, not everyone in a primitive society is going to know all about the myriads of spirits; how best to placate the ghosts; what substances have the most mana; how to determine what infraction of taboo has made a person ill; or what spirit has become so angered as to send a plague upon the people or withhold rain from the withering crops. To guarantee success, one must have specialists, to which a wide variety of names have been given: witch doctors, medicine men, sorcerers, wizards, shamans, priests, and mediums. In general, however, there are two principal types of religious functionaries in primitive religions, the shaman and the priest. Instead of the word "shaman" (a term borrowed from the Tungus of Siberia) we could use "medicine man" or "witch doctor," but these words are emotionally loaded and badly misunderstood. Religious specialists who have been called "medicine men" do much more than prescribe medicines. A "witch doctor" is not a doctor who is a witch, but a person who by any number of means, including divination and

A shaman is considered an expert in manipulating supernatural powers. This shaman of Colombia, South America, cures his patients by spitting tobacco juice on them.

ordeals, is believed to be able to discover who the witches really are.

In many primitive societies there are people who are part-time religious specialists, shamans, functioning more or less on their own. Their approach to the spirits is usually quite direct: by hysterical identification, by becoming the voice of the god, or by calling up the spirit of the dead. This directness of approach is also reflected in the shaman's background. The shaman believes that he has received his power from a direct encounter with the spirit or god. This contrasts with the priest who more frequently depends upon long training, meticulous observance of ritual detail, and social prestige rather than upon ecstatic outbursts of spirit possession. In addition, the shaman usually works directly with a single person or a small group on the basis of an agreed fee. The priest, officially recognized by the society, works for the tribe or community as a whole.

In most primitive communities the shaman is really more important than the priest, for priests exist only in more highly organized societies and then often are restricted to officiating at yearly ceremonies in which everyone participates in a more or less habitual way. But the shaman's role is very different. He must divine the cause of sickness, prescribe the cure, ward off the attacks of evil spirits, track down witches, counter magic with magic. If he is paid enough by the proper persons, he may himself be induced to play the role of the sorcerer. It is just this double role of the shaman which makes him such a power for good or ill. Among the Polar Eskimo, he is regarded as being able to raise or calm a storm, banish or summon the seals, ascend to the sky or descend to the underworld.

The shaman is often an expert in the manipulating of super-natural powers, whether by magic words, powerful charms, fearful fetishes, incredible divination, or frightening seances. Group hypnosis, ventriloquism, and sleight of hand may all play a part. In many parts of the world a shaman must be able to induce hysteria or self-hypnosis and therefore should be the sort of neurotic person who can readily be "entered by his god." This does not mean, of course, that there is no arduous preparation necessary—often consisting of many years as an apprentice—or that he need not be a very clever person. He obviously cannot be stupid if he is to stay in business long, for he will always have competition from other shamans, who are usually only too happy to heap upon him the blame for their own failures, under the condemnation of his being a sorcerer.

It is impossible to draw any hard and fast distinction between shaman and priest, but priests are usually very different types of persons. They are a more formal part of the society and often con-stitute an invisible government. Without them no official divination can be performed, and hence no important governmental action can be carried out.

Becoming a priest in an animistic society is usually no small matter. Among the Ashanti of West Africa, the first year of training is given primarily to ablutions and purification. The second year is dedicated to the study of traditional laws and taboos, including such restrictions as not drinking liquor, gossiping, adjuring one's god to kill someone, or going out at night with other young men. The last year is given to mastering techniques for water divining, incantations, making charms, and hearing and saluting the spirits. In a final ceremony the novitiate shaves all the hair off his body, dances the entire night, and offers a sheep as a sacrifice. He is assisted in his work of divination by women, who act as mediums and utter the words of the god in the midst of hysterical outbursts.

It must not be thought, however, that the highly ecstatic phases of primitive religion are primarily the province of women, who in our culture are thought to be somewhat more emotionally unstable than men and, perhaps, more adept at religious expression. On the con-trary, among the Australian aborigines, men entirely dominate the religious life, and in Africa most of the secret societies are made up of men. Taking the world over, men tend to dominate in religious activities, as they do in most other phases of life, but nowhere do they do so to the complete exclusion of women.

Totemic bark painting
of porcupine by
Australian aborigines.

4 MAGIC AND RITUAL

Having examined the ingredients of primitive religion — the supernatural forces, the techniques for control, and the specialists in spirits —we must now look at the way in which these elements are used in such functions as magic, divination, ordeals, witchcraft, spirit possession, and ceremonialism.

All these various functions are vitally important, but certain aspects of the religious life tend to involve individuals more than the society as a whole. For example, magic, divination, ordeals, witchcraft, and spirit possession are usually the concern of individuals or small groups, and hence the shaman is generally called in. For elaborate ceremonies and the conduct of religious societies, whole clans or tribes of people are often included and these may become the special concern of priests. But there is frequently no clear line of distinction either as to the extent of the group concerned or as to the specialist who should officiate. A whole tribe may engage in magic to produce rain, or to ensure a bountiful harvest; or it may hire a priest to divine the cause of a plague or to solve a crime by staging elaborate ordeals.

If we are to understand fully the real functioning of primitive religious systems, we should recognize the contrast between first, the personal, and frequently selfish, anti-social function of animistic religion as often directed by the medicine man; and second, the group conduct of religious affairs, usually led by a priest. These are not watertight categories. Healing ceremonies and fertility rites, neither of which are anti-social, may be conducted either by the shaman or priest.

Navaho medicine man, in ceremonial hogan above, makes preparations
for sand painting to be used in a five night Holy Way healing ritual
for sick infant. Navahos believe illness to be the result of
an attack by one of the Holy People—a ghost or witch.

Design nears completion. A different sand painting is used on
each of the five nights, after
which it is destroyed and the sand
removed from the ceremonial hogan.

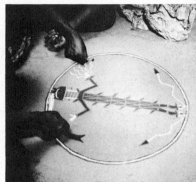

Intricate design of sand
painting begins to take
shape, at left, and above.

Painting completed, medicine man
begins chant and hand trembling
divination to discover cause of
illness, left. Mother and child sit
on sand painting in final ritual.

Magic: White and Black

In order to guarantee a plentiful harvest some tribes of East Africa insist that a woman who has borne many children must sow the grain. To be sure of rain, some South African peoples sprinkle water from a sacred gourd, and a powerful medicine man summons the wind by waving a hyena's tail. Do these people believe that there is any spirit at work in the woman, the gourd, or the tail? Not at all! Magic does not depend upon spirit influences, but upon the potency of contagion and imitation. It is based on two assumptions. The first is that those things that have been in contact with each other continue to affect each other, even at a distance, or after physical association has ended. This is not unlike the idea of mana passing as an electric charge from one object to another. The concept of contagion in magic explains why some people in Cuba will bathe the body of a sick person and then throw the water into the street. They believe that the first person who steps on the wet road will carry away the disease with him, making possible the recovery of the first victim. In this instance the illness is believed to pass first to the water and then to the passerby.

The second principle of magic is that like produces like, so-called imitative magic. It is on the basis of this idea that the Hottentots of Southwest Africa traditionally carried out their annual ceremony to guarantee rain. The people gathered on the bank of a dry watercourse, bringing quantities of milk, and pregnant cows and ewes. The animals were cooked for a great feast. Then, after due preparation, the uteri were held over a flame of sacred fire built on the river bank from which a special channel ran down to the stream bed. As the uteri were pierced, milk was poured onto the flames, the two fluids together flowing onto the fire and down into the stream bed, producing billows of smoke. By imitation, the Hottentots were inducing rain. The smoke represented the clouds; the liquid poured on the fires and into the stream bed was the rain; and the milk and uteri were the symbols of fertility, the results of past rains and the guarantee of future abundance.

But magic is often not merely contagious or imitative; it may be a blend of both principles. For example, a sorcerer, if he wishes to harm a man, may surreptitiously procure a bit of the man's hair, a nail filing, or some food that has been left uneaten. Over these are recited the proper magic formulae, and then the sorcerer may either bury them in the ground to procure the slow death of his victim, or burn them in a hot fire to strike the poor man with instant, torturing death. The little bit of substance previously in touch with the man's body still works its contagious effect. The burying or burning by imitation produces the desired result.

Magic is the Jekyll and Hyde of primitive religion, for it knows no morality. It may be used to procure good, in which case we can call it white magic, or it may produce harm, in which instance we usually say that it is black. But the same magic may be white or black, depending upon who is affected. The man who concocts a magic potion and hides it in a pot in his field in order to protect the crop from thieves is performing white magic for himself, but the thief who falls under the spell of the magic and dies has suffered from black magic.

A man is not, however, helpless in the face of a magic threat. If a Haida Indian of British Columbia learned that a sorcerer had snatched a bit of his clothing and had buried it beside a corpse in order to bring on agonizing death, there was still hope. He could have a little image of himself made by another medicine man, and then place it beneath a small waterfull. The magic was supposed to flow off him even as the water flowed over the tiny image. The outcome of magic depends primarily on the resourcefulness and reputation of the medicine man.

The animist finds in magic a sense of mastery and a capacity to deal with the forces around him. Moreover, even though his magic may sometimes fail, he is convinced that it usually works. His father, grandfather, and his ancestors as far back as anyone can remember, had confidence in just such practices. If magic worked for them, then it will do so for him.

Divination

Being able to divine the future and pierce the veil of the unknown has always intrigued men, and they have used all sorts of methods in their attempts. Some of the techniques employed by the ancient Incas of Peru to apprehend the future are still used by many modern-day Quechuas. They include the interpretation or analysis of: dreams, the twitching of muscles, the flight of birds, the position of stones, the shape of a column of smoke, the number of corn kernels in random heaps, the patterns of blood vessels in inflated lungs of sacrificed llamas, and the distribution of a spider's legs, knocked off by the blow of a stick. Still other interpretative devices may be mentioned. The Bushmen of South Africa observe the behavior of

Letting an evil spirit escape from
a body sometimes requires
drastic methods.
New Guinea tribesmen, above,
keep vigil around sick man
punctured by an arrow.

Magic symbols,
music, and dance are
also enlisted by animists in times of
illness. A group of Choco Indians,
below, and right, are shown
trying to effect a cure.

a praying mantis; a termite's choice of sticks to feed on, or the effect of benge poison given to chickens are analyzed by the Azande Congolese; while the position of pairs of matched bamboo sticks cast on the ground is important in Indonesia. But there are many other methods: cards, numbers, casting of dice, tea leaves, lines in the hand, livers of sacrifices, and so it goes, on and on. There is no limit.

There are three principal types of information that primitive peoples seek. First and foremost they want to determine the unknown causes of the calamities of plague, drouth, sickness, and death. This is especially important when people believe that there is no such thing as *natural* illness or death. If a person only becomes ill because someone is working magic against him or is eating away his soul, or because a spirit has become angry with him for having broken some taboo, then the most important thing one can do is to find out who or what is responsible.

When a child becomes sick in a Vietnamese household, the first question asked is "Why?" Is it a paternal aunt who died without having children and is now seeking to kidnap the spirit of the child? Or is it just that grandfather's spirit wants his bones moved to a drier place? Only the shaman can really determine the cause and so the family must consult him. For a fee—a chicken, some betel nut, a handful of tobacco, or a hamper of rice — he will find the answer. If it is discovered that the paternal aunt is the source of the trouble, then the cure will not be too complicated. The shaman can make a little paper image of the child and burn it, thus sending it on to the spirit world for the peevish old lady to care for. If, however, the condition of grandfather's bones are the difficulty, then once they are dug up and reburied in a sandy, dry spot, the child will immediately get well.

In the second place, diviners try to determine the future, either to forestall some disastrous event or to know whether some particular undertaking is going to turn out well. A bridge is to be built over a stream, but one must not begin it on just any day. Only the medicine man can know what will be the lucky day to begin. Otherwise the bridge is likely to collapse even before it is completed or the termites will eat it up before the next rainy season. The crown prince of Japan is to marry, but diviners must select the proper wedding day or disaster will overtake the throne.

In the third place, diviners are often called on to determine what is happening a great distance away. Certain Mayan shamans are expert in the use of their little rock crystals, which they study in a sort of trance, and declare with astonishing accuracy what is happening at that very moment to their relatives and friends many leagues off.

Divination may be accomplished in one of two ways, either by using some special object, as noted above, or by going into a trance and being possessed by a spirit who communicates, often in obscure phrases, what is likely to happen. Obscurity seems to serve a double purpose. It preserves the reputation of the oracle if events turn out differently from what was presumed, and it also lets the worshiper make his own choice. He can hear what he wants to hear, a convenient technique employed by most diviners.

Ordeals

One of the important functions of magic and spirits is to demonstrate the guilt or innocence of people charged with crimes. Through-

Fiji Islanders value whale teeth, *tabua,* for their inherent power, and a ceremonial gift of *tabua* always accompanies an important event. Fijians, above, are giving *tabua* to the island governor.

Firewalking for a good harvest still survives in Fiji, right. Islanders are standing on rocks hot enough to set the leaves afire.

out central Africa, one of the most common methods of detecting robbers, witches, or murderers consists in administering "the poison cup." When the suspicion of guilt falls upon a particular person, the medicine man is often summoned and ordered to prepare a poison brew of native herbs. The accused must then drink it. If he vomits it, or if, because it is so weak, he manages to outlive its effects, he is declared innocent. But when, as so often happens, he dies, then he is considered guilty, for the spirit of the poison proved the matter. Perhaps the most amazing thing is the fact that many accused people will so readily offer to drink the cup, having implicit faith in its validity. Of course, each man knows that even though seemingly innocent, he may die. But this does not destroy his faith in the ordeal, because he believes that, though he has no knowledge of having perpetrated the crime, he might have done the deed in a dream, or

he might be one of those unfortunate persons who is a witch without knowing it.

Most ordeals, however, do not involve poison, but some more obvious type of "superhuman behavior" with immediately evident reaction. Among the Dahomey, it was the practice to place a red-hot machete on the tongue of the accused to see if blisters resulted, or to make the defendant pick up small seeds from a pot of boiling oil with his bare hands to determine whether the skin would burn. At other times, a hot pepper might be placed under the eyelids and then the eyes would be examined to see if they were inflamed, or a man might be required to kneel on sharp, broken palm nut shells, and then the witch doctor would look to determine whether the skin was cut or abrased.

In Europe, during the Middle Ages, an accused man might be forced to walk barefooted on a red hot plowshare, and Arabs used to touch a white hot knife to the tongue of suspected thieves. It is said that some of these ordeals still continue in some parts of the world. In view of such harsh ordeals, it seems incredible that any person would emerge innocent, but in all cultures it is asserted that innocent people have undergone such trials without the slightest evidence of pain or physical harm. Moreover, competent, reliable observers have fully documented some of these happenings. It would seem, however, far more fair to employ the ordeal reported as formerly held among some of the Lao peoples. When a Lao was accused of being a witch, both the accused and the witch doctor had to sit in pots of boiling oil. The first one to jump out was clubbed to death.

Witchcraft and Sorcery

More to be feared than angry gods, offended spirits, or powerful magic, are the witches—those people who have an unnatural capacity to do harm. In many areas they are believed to be able to fly rapidly through the night, pass mysteriously through closed doors, congregate with other witches in distant lonely places, change themselves instantly into any kind of animal, bird, or reptile, and feed on corpses. In order to harm people, witches may consume their soul-stuff, or life force. A victim gradually becomes ill, his flesh withers away, and at last he dies an awful death. A witch is said to perform this destruction merely by sinister thoughts, for a witch—in contrast with a sorcerer—needs no magic potions, no powerful curses, no slow-acting poisons. The witch employs only psychological means. But what makes a witch even more dangerous is the fact that he or she may not even be aware of being a witch. A person may be found to be a witch when he may never have intended harm to anyone. And in some tribes, the shaman can prove the person was a witch because an autopsy will show strange convolutions of the intestines.

Those who are denounced for being witches are usually anti-social people, the queer people—often psychoneurotic—who tend to behave in such unusual ways that they are suspected of hidden motives. Some people, of course, take a certain pleasure in being known as witches. It gives them a feeling of being able to retaliate against the society that they have already emotionally rejected.

In contrast to the witch, however, the sorcerer is quite another kind of person. He will contrive to do the same evil things as a witch, but by more deliberate means and elaborate techniques. Among the Zulu, in order to kill a man, a sorcerer need only dab his finger in deadly poison and point it at the intended victim. Shortly the man will sicken and die. Among the Australian aborigines, one can accomplish the same purpose by pointing a bone. The Semang point a splinter of bamboo, which by magic they believe they can hurl into the heart of a victim. The sorcerer, depending on his locale, has many other ways of destroying his victims, such as secret curses, smoke from a pot of burning poison blown gently in the direction of a man's hut, or an effigy nailed to a tree in the jungle and pierced through and through with poison-tipped darts.

Once someone discovers that he has been bewitched or cursed, he generally becomes ill and often dies. Moreover, if a man gets sick apparently for no good reason, it is frequently regarded as the best of evidence that someone has cursed him, and his condition rapidly worsens. The truth is that if people actually believe that they are doomed by witchcraft or sorcery, they really become "scared to death." They often refuse to eat and decline to exercise. Since they cannot rid themselves of the sickening fear of death, they die.

The only possible means of escape is through the help of a shaman. He can determine who the witch or sorcerer is and get him to desist by confession of his guilt, or by having him done away with, or the shaman can concoct a medicine that will overcome the witch's spell or the sorcerer's magic. Since in many parts of the world illness is thought to consist of some foreign matter that has gotten into the body, one technique of saving the patient is to let out the spirit of the illness. This may be done by piercing the body with bone or

An important specialist in his animistic society, a Tibetan shaman stands surrounded by his equipment, including characteristic banner or tanka.

bamboo splinters. For severe pains in the head, some peoples are exceedingly clever in trepanning, which consists of cutting a small piece of bone out of the skull, just enough to let the spirit escape. Of course, sometimes the shaman has some really good remedies—primitive peoples discovered quinine, cascara, cocaine, and morphine. Moreover, he is occasionally highly proficient at setting bones or relieving the pain of sprains, but a large per cent of a shaman's remedies are purely psychosomatic. A clever operator can build up quite a reputation for cures. As his reputation grows and people's faith in him increases, so does his capacity for effecting more and more spectacular results.

A Belgian Congo woman,
believed to be "possessed,"
awaits the shaman.

One thing that makes primitive medical practice so psychologically useful is that in most instances medicines are specially compounded for the individual patient. The shaman may try to use only rare substances, such as ground lions' teeth, powdered butterflies, pieces of a liver of a witch, chips of dragon bones, and dust from mummies; and he often personalizes his medicine by making them specifically applicable to the patient. For example, among the San Blas Indians of Panama, a medicine man will bring a little wooden doll along with his medicines, concocted of such things as mountain herbs, sharks' teeth, porpoise bones, and shellfish. After the patient explains precisely in what part of his body he has pain, the shaman will scrape off some tiny shavings from the doll at the corresponding place and add these to the medicine so that the substances will know just where to go in the body in order to do their work of healing.

The introduction of modern medicine by missionaries has not put the shaman completely out of business, for animists interpret sickness quite differently from the way we do. The Azande of the Sudan and the Belgian Congo, for example, look at illness something like hunting, in which the man who throws the first spear into an animal must share the meat with the man who throws the second spear. This analogy applies specifically to accidents. If a man has been killed by an elephant, the elephant is considered the first spear. But the witch who arranged for the victim to be just at that point at that time is believed to have hurled the second spear. Similarly in the case of illness, there may be two factors: the infection, sore, or cancerous growth on the one hand, and the evil influences of witchcraft and magic on the other. If the government or missionary doctor has diagnosed the physical cause and prescribed the right medicines for a person to get well, the difficult problem is only half solved. The doctor has not eliminated the influence of the witch who brought on the sickness and who, if not exposed, will only continue to make the victim ill.

From Vision Quests to Spirit Possession

For some people the highest form of religion is to be found in ecstatic experiences in which they see visions, fall into rapture, or experience possession by their god. Among the Indians of the Great Plains, the Crows were a typical vision-seeking people. Each man had to have a vision of his guardian spirit, usually of some animal, which became his protector and source of his power. To obtain a vision, however, was not easy, for it meant suffering cold, going without food and water, or enduring self-inflicted torture. But without such a vision a man was doomed to be a neglected nobody in a society that placed unusual emphasis upon individual daring and heroic exploits.

In voodoo worship in Haiti, the focus of attention is not the weird fetishes, the fearful orgies, or the noisy dancing. What really matters to the worshiper is that ecstatic moment in the night-long dance when at last the exhausted celebrant feels that his god is "riding" him. This is the ecstacy of voodoo.

As a result of individual and group hypnosis, many worshipers are able to do utterly incredible things. They can throw themselves high into the air and repeatedly let themselves crash to the ground. They speak in strange tongues, walk on burning coals, chew glass, and thrust knives and daggers into their cheeks and tongues — all without suffering any apparent permanent injury.

Other peoples desire their ecstatic experiences in a more controlled manner like the ascetic who seeks rapture in seclusion, the Yogi who is looking for identification through exercise and meditation, and the exhausted pilgrim who travels the last ten miles on hands and knees. All seek to be acknowledged by their gods, to be known and to know and to be enraptured by sight and feeling.

Ritual and Ceremonies

Of all spectacles none is more gripping than a religious drama in which men are pitted against the gods or entreat the spirits for the blessings without which life cannot go on. It is by means of elaborate ceremonies that many of the world's peoples act out their relationships to their deities, induce them to remove barrenness from women and fields, and feel the participation of spirits and ghosts in human affairs. While the secret mysteries are being depicted and the mystic symbols are being exhibited, all the participants thrill to the sense of their oneness with the deity and each other. Their shared knowledge has welded them closer and closer together.

Rituals can be performed for almost any purpose: to propitiate the spirits, to prepare for war, to procure heads in revenge for recent deaths, to signal adulthood, to consecrate marriage, to bring rain, to halt a thunderstorm, to crown a king, and to send the dead on to the spirit world. The most common, and perhaps most important ceremonies for most peoples, center about times of crisis in their lives, especially birth, puberty, marriage, and death. It is on these occasions that special rites must be performed if a person is to pass through such crises with the full protection and blessing of the supernatural world.

In some societies the rites of birth begin when first a woman discovers that she is pregnant. A Semang woman, for example, must be sure to procure for her child a soul, which resides in a bird. Accordingly, she goes to the nearest tree of a species after which she herself is named and she decorates it with leaves and flowers. When the soul-bird alights, it is immediately killed and eaten by the mother. Only in this way can the child be guaranteed of having a soul. The mother, however, must also observe certain taboos, for she must not eat any flesh of a large fish, monitor lizards, squirrels, wild boars, or any animal killed with a bow and arrow.

Birth itself is often surrounded by all kinds of elaborate precautions, including long ceremonies conducted by medicine men, extensive auguries, and the sympathetic wailing of neighbors. One element in birth, however, seems to involve special attention. It is the umbilical cord — the symbol of life itself. In Dahomey when the umbilical cord finally falls off, it is buried at the foot of a palm tree, which the child must respect and protect throughout his life. The Baganda in East Africa also preserve the umbilical cord. After three months it is placed in a waterproof basket containing a mixture of beer, milk, and water. If the cord floats, the child is regarded as legitimate, but if it sinks, the child is disowned and the mother flogged. In either event the small piece of cord is carefully kept. The king's cord is, of course, highly important, and the "Keeper of the King's Umbilical Cord" is one of the two major posts in the royal court.

Fathers are also involved in birth rituals. A number of societies, including some in southeastern Europe and many in South America,

New Mexican Indians invoke the spirits for a
good harvest in this timeless ceremonial corn dance.

Australian totemic rite at sacred tree is
performed to increase the supply of salmon, below.

practice the couvade, a period of time during which the father of a newborn child goes to bed. Among the Witoto, a jungle tribe at the headwaters of the Amazon, fathers must not work, hunt, or even touch their weapons till the baby's navel heals.

In some societies even the gods are handy in training children. A Zuni mother who is having difficulty in making junior behave, may call on the Atoshle, impersonations of the gods, who carry giant yucca plant leaves and wield large stone knives with which they are reputed to cut off the heads of naughty children. Exploits of the Atoshle make hair-raising stories, and though mother may be able gradually to calm junior's fears, she can be sure he will think twice before he continues any defiant misbehavior.

Puberty is often regarded as a time of great spiritual danger. In preparation for this, some tribes conduct elaborate initiation ceremonies, including isolation in a ceremonial village deep in the jungle; circumcision for boys and a corresponding rite of clitorectomy for girls; ordeals of fasting; strenuous feats; and instruction in tribal lore. Very often at such ceremonies initiates are shown grotesque masks of the spirits and mystic symbols of fertility. They listen to bull-roarers, the voices of the gods, and are required to participate in sex acts as proof of their adult status. If, as is not infrequently the case, a young boy or girl dies as the result of exposure, abuse, or infection from wounds, the community only learns that a spirit has taken him away. (It should be noted that the impact of modern ways is rapidly modifying many of these practices over much of the world.)

In many societies marriage is usually regarded as more of a social and economic arrangement between families than as a religious institution, but if a marriage is to be successful, the appropriate spirits must be consulted. How would Dahomean parents know that the boy they had decided upon for their girl was the right one if they did not first consult the spirits? Similarly the boy's parents will do the same, and if either young person has become a devotee of a cult god, further consultations must take place. If all the gods and especially the ancestors of the two families are not satisfied, such a marriage is thought to be doomed to failure. Certain Asian peoples observe similar customs.

The most important rites center about death, for the souls of those who have just departed this life are regarded as highly dangerous. If a man was bad before he died, how much more evil he can be as a spirit! What is more, he is unlikely to be as happy as a ghost as he was on earth, and hence jealousy or peevishness may make him utterly untrustworthy. Therefore, three things must be done: (1) He must be

Christian and animistic practices entwine in Mexican cemetery,
where cactus, source of cheap liquor, is planted to provide drink for dead.

Grief is the same the world over. In the Congo, ritual lamentations shared
by the community help sustain parents of a dead child, below.

avoided, and it is not easy to avoid the unseen. (2) He must be helped on his way (sky rockets are used by Indians in southern Mexico and Guatemala to speed the spirits on their journey). (3) He must be kept contented in the spirit world. The San Blas Indians try to accomplish the latter by faithful offerings of food for the dead, placed in tiny thatched huts built over each grave.

Mourning for the dead is a problem in all societies, for the first impulse of bereaved persons is identification with those who have passed on. Some peoples engage in cruel self torture, inflicting deep wounds and causing copious bleeding. Another symbol of identification with the dead involves seclusion, either complete isolation or heavy veiling. Such separation from the rest of society seems to have a double purpose, for it is thought by some peoples not only to symbolize one's affinity with the dead, but also to prevent the contagion of death from spreading to others. Still another means of mourning is distinctive dress, blackened countenance, or symbolic tattoos. However, despite the endless rites of wailing and crying, the numerous gifts to the departed ghosts, and the frequent sacrifices, the period of mourning must ultimately result in people's being identified more with the living than with the dead, or mass suicides would result. To help in this process a person's friends are called in to participate, and it is this social fortification, aided by religious sanctions, which carries the grief-stricken person through his troubled days.

The actual disposal of the body is a matter of special concern in many societies. The Motilones of Colombia bury it right in the dirt floor of a hut and then after a few months dig it up, clean the bones of any clinging, rotten flesh, wrap up the bones in a fetal position (that the spirit may be properly reborn), and hide the bundle away in a dry cave in the mountains. Other peoples, such as the Masai of East Africa and the Parsees of India have traditionally exposed bodies to the birds and the elements. But most peoples treat the body with some care, either dressing it up in its finest apparel, often surrounded by the tools and jewels of this life, or arranging to provide it with some helpful token by which it may make the great migration to the other world. The ancient Greeks put a coin in the mouth of the dead as payment to the ferryman on the river Styx, and Fijians enclose in a man's coffin a lock of his wife's hair as a gift to the giant who guards the approaches to the next world.

From birth to death the animist is wrapped up in religious observance. In times of prosperity and of disaster, he seeks an avenue of approach to the forces that he believes control him and his destiny.

Unusual three-headed totem pole from Canada carved by Haida Indians.

5 BASIC ANIMIST BELIEFS

Even though animists cannot cite the articles of their creed, they do have a set of beliefs or assumptions. In fact, many of these beliefs are very subtle interpretations of nature and life itself, and hence, despite the strangeness of their concepts, animists should not be considered as possessing minds essentially different from our own. What makes their behavior so distinct from ours and their ways of thinking so inexplicable to us is that they look at life very differently. A man is as he thinks, and the animist does not think our thoughts. He has his own, and they must be understood if we are to understand him.

In the following generalizations about animistic beliefs, we must recognize that there are many exceptions in individual groups and that some of these "beliefs" are only implied in behavior and not specifically held by the people themselves. To try to summarize animistic beliefs is therefore somewhat misleading. There are, however, enough common assumptions — especially in Negro Africa for which this summary is primarily applicable — to examine profitably in order to understand why people do as they do.

Unity of All Nature

The first assumption of most animists is that reality is all of one piece. That is to say, there is not the same water-tight distinction between human beings and animals, or between animate and inanimate existence. Animals may be ancestors of men, people may change into animals, trees and stones may possess souls, and the mana of a stick may be transferred to a man. In fact, in some groups, almost every object in the universe is viewed as possessing some amount of life force — the spiritual, nonmaterial substance without which nothing could exist and that in reality is its true character and the secret of its power. This life force, or soul-stuff, exists in greater concentrations in famous men, strong charms, revered fetishes, and powerful gods. In essence the force is the same everywhere, it is only distributed in different quantities. The secret of strength, fame, and riches is the possession of a great amount of this life force, which can be acquired by various means, as by inheritance, by white magic, or by robbing other men, animals, and spirits of what is theirs.

This relationship is not only spatial with the animate and inanimate world that surrounds an animist, but also temporal with his ancestors who have gone on before, and with his descendants who will follow. He is merely a link in the chain of existence, a transmitter of life force, a momentary depository of some of the soul-stuff that permeates the universe. This relationship with the past and future is no mere historical perspective. In fact, it is not historical at all in the sense that we use history — as a succession of events. Everything is essentially contemporaneous. The souls of the dead still exist and participate in a man's life, protecting him from danger and keeping him faithful to the traditions. Each man must in turn pass on this vital force to his descendants, therefore, he must have children who can in turn honor him in the spirit world, and for whom he can in turn be a protecting, or haunting ghost. There is also another phase to this relationship with the dead. It involves strict observance of ancient customs, for radical change would certainly annoy, if not shock, the dead. If the spirits of the dead are to approve of the living, they must feel at home. Change of a conspicuous kind is, therefore, suspect and progress tends to be ruled out.

Almost as important as his spatial identification with the nature around him, or temporal association with ancestors and descendants, is the animist's understanding of himself as psychologically akin to the inhabitants of the spirit world. This does not mean that the average animist would claim to be divine, but he does not hesitate to deify great kings or to think that powerful sorcerers are really not men, but are disguised inhabitants from the spirit world. He believes that men can be possessed by spirits, become their voices, and receive their visions. He is certain that dreams permit him, or the shaman, to be transported into the very realm of the demons, and that there is no activity of which spirits are capable that some men cannot also engage in.

This does not mean that animists confuse people, spirits, and ghosts.

Tattooed symbols
bring good luck or
ward off evil.
Tattooed Mentaweier
of East Indies, left,
is distinguished as well
by the headdress
of the unmarried.

They do not. But, nevertheless, they behave as though the differences by which one may distinguish people, spirits, and ghosts are really quite superficial. Underlying these more obvious differences is an essential oneness. This is not dissimilar to our own understanding of the psychological unity of mankind, for despite vast differences of race and culture, we believe that all people are essentially similar in their psychological make-up. The animist extends this concept of unity to include the spirit world, where gods and spirits, ghosts and men, all exhibit the same fundamental characteristics and capacities for love and hate, generosity and miserliness, altruism and self-interest.

Religion Without Ethics

One result of believing that gods and spirits are at heart only like men is that the animist's religion is essentially non-ethical. To him, religion is primarily a technique for procuring the best advantage in the power struggle in the spirit world. It may very well be that some ghosts, such as Sir Ghost among the Manus, insist on upright behavior, at least as far as work and payments of debts are concerned. Other spirits may be offended because of adultery, incest, or thievery. In fact, the spirits may be counted on to promote the social values of the group, even to the detriment of the individuals. Even some of the most mischievous or meanest spirits will see to it that people conform to the mores of the tribe. The jinns see to this in North Africa and the thunder gods of Dahomey are bent on social propriety. But custom may not be essentially ethical in the sense that it is socially beneficial. Karei, the thunder god of the Semang, fiercely punishes the violation of taboos, which include such acts as theft or murder, but which also prohibit familiarity with one's mother-in-law, killing a sacred black wasp or certain birds, mocking a tame or helpless animal, having sexual intercourse in the daytime, combing one's hair during a thunderstorm, and playing with bird's eggs.

Many animists believe that the fate that one suffers in the next world depends very largely upon how good or bad one has been in this one. However, the Bakauna of Melanesia have no idea of punishment or reward in the next world, and many other peoples have thought that one's destiny depended essentially on the manner in which one happened to die. The ancient Aztecs, for example, believed that most dead people went to Mictlan, a sort of dreary place of eternal cold and dampness. Those who drowned or were struck dead by light-

This Balinese boy's unshaved forelock and phylactery protect him from illness.   The forelock will never be cut.

ning, or died because of dropsy or leprosy, entered Tlalocan, the abode of the rain gods, to enjoy perpetual summer and all they wanted to eat and drink. Those who died in war or childbirth or who were sacrificed to the gods, passed immediately into the most attractive heaven, where they flitted about like hummingbirds.

In the island of Tikopia, the gods take a very active part in preaching morality to the people through persons who are believed to utter exhortations on behalf of the gods, but the usual themes are to reduce quarreling in the families and to practice birth control, for the lack of a food supply on the island makes such admonitions a reflection of the social conscience.

Certainly one cannot say that animistic religions are anti-ethical, despite some orgiastic sex debauches that may involve whole villages at funerals or in fertility ceremonies. These sanctioned violations of regular conduct are thought to be required if life is to continue and strength is to be increased. The gods do endorse the social values of the tribe — whether ethical or unethical — and thus indirectly they may be credited with certain ethical standards. However, it is no anomaly for the animist to turn for religious guidance to the most immoral man of the village, a medicine man whose reputation for antisocial acts may include everything from rape to murder. What matters for the animist is that this person knows the secrets of spiritual power. He is the expert in manipulating the spirits, and why should the spirits, who are themselves often quite evil, be concerned about the morality of one who directs the ritual or prescribes the magic cure?

This character of animistic religion shoves the door wide open to gross abuse. When one realizes that the possibilities for error are almost unlimited and that the results of such confident error are so devastating, it is not difficult to realize how throughout history the worst things ever done on a large scale by otherwise decent people have been done in the name of religion.

Control of Spirit Power

One basic assumption that is implied in all animistic practices is the controllability of the spirit power. If only one knows the right formulae, the spirit world can be made to do one's bidding, whether for good or for evil. The animist is not concerned about seeking the will of his god, but in compelling, entreating, or coercing his god to do his will.

One last tenet of animistic belief must be emphasized, namely, that religion is all-embracing in its affect upon life. From conception to death, from morning till night, from springtime until harvest, and from the start of any enterprise (whether building a house or hunting for hippos) until its end, supernatural forces are present and must be properly dealt with, or failure is inevitable. As animists come more and more into contact with the secularized views of urban centers, religion begins to lose its hold. The gods are no longer there to be feared and the old restraints, which bolstered the social life of the village, disappear. But though an animist may lose his gods, he does not lose his basic orientation — that life should serve selfish ends.

Faith and Skepticism

One may reasonably ask why animists have apparently never begun to study their own beliefs, or to be critical toward them. But, before we judge them too harshly, we must remind ourselves that rarely do any people become self-critical. The classical Greeks were one rare exception and the Western scientific world still follows in their tradition in this respect. Many primitive systems of belief, of which the ancient Greek and the Polynesian are the most famous, have been quite unintentionally developed in the very process of elaborating a system of myths. This involves fascinating projections of a people's own unconcious rationalization, as when the Masai insist that stealing cattle is not bad, for their god gave them all the cattle in the world; other people should not exhibit such cupidity in trying to hold on to their cattle instead of letting the divinely appointed owners go off with them. Rationalizing by means of religion is a favorite device for all sorts of persons, but thinking rationally about one's own religion is a rare phenomenon.

There has been a tendency for some persons to think that animists do not really have a religion because there is no body of formal doctrine to which all the people subscribe. Where there is no formalized creed, there is supposedly no faith and no belief. But this is not so. Creeds generally contain only those articles that a man thinks he should assert positively against those who think otherwise. A person's most practical and most personal beliefs are those on which he acts without question, ones that have never been regarded as even open to question. This means that just because an animist cannot describe his beliefs or defend his "theology" it is no sign that he has no religious beliefs. The truth of the matter is that religious concerns occupy far more of his attention and involve far more of his life than is the

Kenya Masai, right, burn a sacred live tree whose smoke and flame are believed to bring good luck.

A village in the Belgian Congo, left, offers a thanksgiving ceremonial for UNICEF aid.

case with many Christians, who have often succeeded quite well in restricting religion to perfunctory church attendance and to some twinges of conscience over obviously unethical conduct.

On the other hand, one must not get the impression that all animists are deeply committed to their religious beliefs. There is almost the same degree of variability as among ourselves. Much depends upon just how religion-centered a particular tribe is. Religion rests rather lightly on a Polynesian group, for example, but a Melanesian tribe is given over almost entirely to magic rites and the propitiation of spirits. Whether a person is highly religious in certain animistic cultures depends very much upon personal suggestibility and the capacity for certain wildly emotional outbursts and raptures. There are, of course, some skeptics in almost all societies, but in general there are fewer in primitive cultures than in our own. Part of our own modern faith is the validity of skepticism — the cult of agnosticism.

Weaknesses in Animistic Beliefs

When confronted with the claims of Christianity, or even of other major religions, animistic beliefs have usually proved to be weak. They have capitulated to organized religious systems far more quickly than the more elaborate religions have given in to each other. There are

several reasons for this inherent weakness in the primitive religions.

In the first place, there is no fundamental moral basis in animism. Without this essentially ethical outlook no religion can expect to withstand competition from a religion that proclaims a moral basis for conduct. The sentiments of religious reverence and social morality are too closely related to be neatly and permanently isolated from each other. On the other hand, a religious belief that is scientifically preposterous may still enjoy a long and comfortable life, for worshipers seem quite capable of suspending the scientific part of their minds while worshiping. However, they cannot suspend judgment on what is morally contemptible while at the same time being challenged by a deep religious sentiment that is basically good and just. As in the case of the religions of ancient Greece and Rome, the vulnerable point was the traditional mythology, filled with the absurd moral antics of the gods. By the process of allegorizing, an attempt was made to adjust such myths to the science of the day, but they could not be refurbished to meet the moral challenge posed by the Christians.

In the second place, animism provides no satisfactory answer to the question of the meaning of life and the significance of history. If behind each individual there stand the spirit beings and the dead — all interested merely in enforcing the customs of the society — the entire orientation of the society becomes focused on the past. The only real answer that people can give as to why they do things in a particular way is, "our fathers did it that way." This approach does not remain forever satisfying to people who are confronted with new and different possibilities. Merely looking back does not provide sufficient inspiration for the future. Where there is no vision of a different future there is no opportunity for progress and little sense of purpose.

A third weakness is that often the religious leaders — shamans, sorcerers, or mediums — are the "lunatic fringe" of society. They are often psychotic, mentally deranged, emotionally unstable. Although they are often very clever people, they do not provide the kind of constructive leadership that any society needs. A person who is convinced that he can make himself into a bear or a wolf is not the type of individual who is likely to be of real help to a society in competition with a materialistic, modern world.

A fourth liability in primitive beliefs is the undue emphasis upon the physiological and infantile in religious practice. The constant concern with segregation of women during menstruation, bloody sacrifices, scarification, operations on the genital organs, preservation of skulls, fertility orgies, and ritual prostitution are essentially physiological and infantile in their orientation. Though such practices may appeal to people for a time because of their very elemental and mystic character, they are not fully satisfying, since they are essentially beneath man's capacity for religious expression.

Though primitive religions do tend to help men adjust to the universe by giving them some sense of control, thus eliminating certain elements of fear, they do not actually solve this problem of meeting life's crises. The trouble is that elemental fear of the immediate, primary danger is only transferred to a secondary agent of concern, namely, the spirits themselves, who cannot ultimately be trusted. Though fear demands a more highly charged response than does trust, nevertheless, in the ultimate analysis, the fear of largely irresponsible spirits is no competition to trust in a loving, heavenly Father.

But a more serious deficiency than failure to solve the problem of fear is the inability of animism to deal effectively in so many instances with the needs of the social group. Primitive religions directly and indirectly encourage many anti-social practices: fear of witches, suspicions of black magic, loss of life through initiation ceremonies, headhunting, the use of erratic divination for making social decisions, and dependence upon emotionally unstable persons who may dominate not only the religious activities of the group but also the political and economic areas of life as well.

*Carved wooden
fetish figure from
the Congo.*

6 THE IMPACT OF CHRISTIANITY ON THE ANIMISTIC WORLD

The impact of Christianity on the animistic world has been both striking and profound. The Bataks of Sumatra ate the first two missionaries who came to them about a century ago, but now more than one million Batak Christians have their own churches, ministry, and schools. Among the hill tribes of Burma there are more than 200,000 Christians, and in Assam there are well over 175,000 from the many Naga and related tribes of the Himalayan slopes. In the South Pacific whole islands have become Christian communities, of which Fiji and Tonga are perhaps the most noted examples, while in Negro Africa there are literally tens of thousands of churches. In Uganda almost 30 per cent of the population has become related to the Christian church, and in Haiti virtually 10 per cent of the population are turning from voodoo to the evangelical church. As many as 50 per cent of some tribes of the Americas have left their animistic ways to become Christians.

It is true that these groups are often quite small and in comparison with figures of world population these former animists are not numerous. But when the percentage of converts from animistic religions is compared with conversions in the areas of the major non-Christian religions, the contrast is very great. In Thailand, for example, despite intensive missionary work for more than a century, there are still less than one-tenth of one per cent of the Thai who have become Christians. In Japan, Protestant Christians represent less than one-half of one per cent. In fact, in no major pagan region in the so-called "missionary world," apart from aboriginal areas, has Protestant missionary work gained more than one per cent of the population.

Undoubtedly, among former animists, conversion may not have

always sprung from purely religious motives. Sometimes people are induced to identify themselves with the church because of the special benefits that they think they will derive from such an association: free education, better health, more money, and enhanced prestige. But no amount of discounting people's real spiritual convictions can ever explain the fundamental changes that have occurred in the lives of hundreds of thousands of animistic peoples. Fifteen years ago in the region of Oxchuc in southern Mexico, the Tzeltals were a depressed, demoralized, and degenerate group, with one man in ten practicing black magic; with fear of evil spirits thwarting any attempt to improve the people's lot; and with constant drunken festivals, sponsored in the name of religion, producing moral chaos. The people were then brought the message of Jesus Christ, who gave life that they might have life. A few accepted, and despite severe persecution, including both loss of property and lives, the witness of God's power was so manifest that this little body of believers has now grown to include more than five thousand Indians.

In one region of the Belgian Congo dominated by the "poison cup," where suspected witches were brutally beaten to death, where the witchdoctor and sorcerer have held tyrannical control for generations, and where the spirits of the dead and the power of fetishes have dictated the most minute actions of individuals and every decision of the tribes, within a period of ten years the number of Christians increased from about seven thousand to more than twenty-seven thousand.

We ask the question, "How can one account for such a response to the story of God's love as expressed in Jesus Christ?" Certainly the mere inadequacies of animistic beliefs alone cannot explain this turning to Christ. Rather, the reasons are to be found in the very nature of the Christian message and faith, and its particular appeal to animistic peoples.

The Bible

Throughout the world the Scriptures, at least in part, have been published in over 1,100 languages, a majority of which are spoken by so-called animistic peoples. However, the mere fact of this tremendous undertaking of translating, publishing, and distributing the Bible (a task in which missions and the Bible Societies have had such a large share) does not adequately account for the receptivity that so many peoples have had for the Scriptures when they were well trans-

Witch doctors bow to change in modern Africa. At left, a woman disposes of her paraphernalia in a public ceremony in Kenya in which 400 witch doctors renounced their craft. Below, a witch doctor watches Western trained medical technicians at work.

lated into their own tongue. Rather, it is the distinctive, unique character of the Bible that is so largely responsible. It is so realistic, so down-to-earth in its imagery and treatment of human problems, so "unphilosophical" in its vocabulary, but so profoundly moral and ethical in its message. All this has appealed strongly to animistic peoples. Moreover, the culture reflected in the Bible, especially in the Old Testament, is so much like that of many peoples of Africa and Asia today that one West African said, "That's us right there." The animist sees in the Scriptures an undeniably accurate picture of his own heart.

Revelation of God in Christ

If an animist has one god higher and greater than the rest of his multitude of spirit beings, that god is always too impersonal and distant to care for human beings. To the Kaka of the Cameroun, God is

a spider. To be sure, he created man, but that is no reason for loving him, for he is like a spider, not like man.

In Christ, God has a face. The story of Jesus, his life, death and resurrection, has led thousands to realize that no man ever loved as this one who revealed the very heart of God. In Christ, God is no longer distant, unseen and unseeing. He enters right into the midst of everyday life, where he seeks men to be reconciled to him, to be his children and his friends.

The New Way of Life

Many animists have been genuinely challenged by the possibility of a new way of life as Christians. To be sure, the message of the gospel has not always been understood, and the "new way" has often been confused with some of the superficial aspects of "Western behavior," clothes, haircuts, marriage customs, bicycles, flashlights, and a thousand other things. But shining through all of this irrelevant westernization, many sensitive animists have seen what is meant by "old things pass away and everything becomes new." As a result they have come to know by experience the meaning of unqualified devotion to God, holy living in the world, and selfless service to others.

New Guinea patient,
inadequately treated
by witch doctor,
receives further attention
from missionary doctor, left.

Old Sumatra Batak tombstone
and new Christian marker
symbolize struggle between
Christianity and animism.

The Fellowship of Believers

Primitive societies of the world are being badly disrupted by the rapid social changes of the twentieth century. Tribal life is breaking down as thousands of men leave their villages to find work in the cities. Moral standards are disintegrating because the powerful social and religious controls of village life no longer apply in the relatively organized mass of humanity that lives in the squalid slums, the shanty towns, and the mining compounds. People are left rootless and drifting in a bitterly competitive and hostile world.

The Church of the Living God is the only real answer to the breakdown of tribal life. It provides a new social unit based not on the old patterns of clan and village, but on a new pattern of common love for the Master, common service, and common worship.

In essence the impact of Christianity has meant a change *from fear to faith.* One reason — often the first and most important — given by former animists for their conversion has been that Christ meant freedom from fear. Even the shamans complain that once a man becomes a believer in Christ he is no longer subject to the curses of black magic, nor are the evil spirits able to attack him. Becoming a Christian has meant a step from basic mistrust of an irresponsible spirit world to growing confidence in an eternal God.

READING LIST

Good, William J. *Religion Among the Primitives*. Glencoe, Ill.: Free Press, 1951. Treats the economic and social problems associated with primitive religions.

Howells, William. *Heathens: Primitive Man and His Religions*. New York: Doubleday & Company, Inc., 1948. A light, popular introduction to the field.

Kluckhohn, Clyde. *Mirror for Man*. New York: McGraw-Hill Book Company, Inc., 1949. A non-technical approach to anthropology.

Kroeber, Alfred L. *Anthropology*. New York: Harcourt, Brace and Company, rev. ed., 1948. A historical approach to many anthropological concerns.

Murdock, George Peter. *Our Primitive Contemporaries*. New York: The Macmillan Company, 1934. Short descriptions of the characteristics of several representative societies.

Nida, Eugene Albert. *Customs and Cultures: Anthropology for Christian Missions*. New York: Harper & Brothers, 1934. Non-technical work describing human customs all over the world and their significance to missions.

——— *God's Word in Man's Language*. New York: Harper & Brothers, 1934. An account of the communication of the gospel to non-Western peoples.

Service, Elman Rogers. *Profile of Primitive Cultures*. New York: Harper & Brothers, 1958. Sketches the range and variety of cultural types and experiences.

Acknowledgements

American Museum of Natural History: 1, 3, 32, 33, 59; Australian News and Information Bureau: 11, 21, 31; British Information Service: 57, 61 left; Belgian Government Information Center: 43, 48 bottom, 56; Frink from Monkmeyer: 19, 27; Philip Gendreau: 22; Richard Harrington: 50; Richard Harrington from Black Star: 8; Japan Tourist Association: 16; Jurg Klages from Black Star: 13; Linaris from Monkmeyer: 6, 7 top; Luenberger from Black Star: 61 right; A. Maaks from Black Star: 36, 62; Fosco Maraini from Monkmeyer: 7 bottom, 42; Herbert Matter from Black Star: 46 top; Mondiale from Black Star: 23, 46 bottom; Monkmeyer: 52; Pan-Asia Photos from Black Star: 9; Marita Pease from Monkmeyer: 48 top; Kurt Severin from Black Star: 29, 36; Tiers from Monkmeyer: 26, 53, 63; Wide World Photos: 2; Rob Wright from Black Star: 38, 39.

COVER AND FORMAT BY WARREN JOHNSON.